G000155032

Grandparent's
Journey with
Autism

AS PUBLISHING

THIS BOOK BELONGS TO

Grandparent's Journey with Autism

=============================

A Grandparent's Guide to Supporting Autistic Grandchildren

AS Publishing

PUBLISHING

 Published by **AS Publishing**

Follow Us to Stay Updated on New Releases

We offer our eBooks for free during the initial launch period. By following us, you will be among the first to know when a new eBook is released and have the opportunity to download it completely free of charge.

Don't miss out on our latest releases! Simply click on the link below, follow us, and stay up-to-date on all of our new eBooks.

amazon.com/author/as-publishing

Attribution: The resources utilized to design this cover were obtained from Pxhere.com.

Disclaimer

This book's instructions, recommendations, or methods are not intended to replace professional medical guidance, diagnosis, or care. The information in this book is only meant to be used for educational purposes; it should not be used as a replacement for professional medical advice from a healthcare provider.

The authors and publisher of this book disclaim any responsibility for any negative effects or outcomes attributable to the use of the knowledge, suggestions, or methods offered in this book. Readers should speak with their doctor before beginning any new health or wellness program.

Despite the fact that the knowledge and research upon which the information in this book is based is up-to-date, medical procedures and recommendations may alter over time.

It is advised that readers seek out additional information and keep current with healthcare trends.

The authors' views are the only ones that are expressed in this book; they do not necessarily represent the publisher's views. The authors and publisher do not endorse or recommend any companies, items, or services that are mentioned in this book.

Despite making every effort to ensure the accuracy and comprehensiveness of the information in this book, the authors and publisher make no promises or representations of any kind, either explicitly or implicitly, regarding the information's suitability, reliability, or availability.

Any risks associated with relying on the information in this book are assumed by the reader.

ISBN: 9798393548889

Contents

> ## The Gift of Love

❖ A Grandparent's Guide to Autism

A grandparent's love is a priceless treasure, a gift that transcends time and space. It is a love that knows no boundaries, one that extends far beyond the limits of blood or kinship. It is a love that is unconditional, unwavering, and infinite. And when a grandchild is diagnosed with autism, that love becomes all the more precious, all the more essential.

Receiving an autism diagnosis can be frustrating, perplexing, or even terrifying for many grandparents. The opportunity to embark on a romantic, educational, and exploratory journey is also presented. It's an opportunity to strengthen your bond with your grandchild, discover the complexity and diversity of the human brain, and advance inclusiveness and tolerance.

The benefits and drawbacks of having a grandchild with autism are discussed in this book.porting your grandchild's development and well-being. We will celebrate the unique strengths and abilities of autistic individuals, and promote a culture of acceptance and inclusion.

We will also address the emotional and practical aspects of navigating this journey, from advocating for systemic change to finding community and support. And throughout it all, we will reiterate the value of love, which serves as the cornerstone of everything we do as grandparents.

Please come and join me as we set off on this voyage. Let's embrace the strength of love to lead us down this path as we celebrate the beauty of diversity. As we will discover, the love of a grandparent is a gift that can change the world.

❖ The Unique Joy and Challenges of Having an Autistic Grandchild

A grandparent's love for their grandchild transcends geography, time, and circumstances. It is a love that endures, even when miles or years separate us from those we cherish. It acts as a daily reminder of how lovely and wonderful life is and makes us joyful and grateful.

And when a grandchild is identified as having autism, that love acquires a new level of significance. For as grandparents of autistic children, we are blessed with a unique opportunity and responsibility. We are expected to appreciate our grandchild's talents and skills, to work through any difficulties that may occur, and to fight for a society that values and accepts everyone, neurodiversity and all.

We shall examine the benefits and difficulties of raising an autistic grandchild in this book. We will discuss instances of love, bravery, and tenacity while also providing suggestions and tactics for helping your grandchild and family. We will celebrate the unique perspectives and talents of autistic individuals, and promote a culture of acceptance and inclusion.

Along the way, from adjusting to the initial diagnosis to creating a network of resources and support, we will also talk about the emotional and practical aspects of navigating this trip. And throughout it all, we will reiterate the value of love, which serves as the cornerstone of everything we do as grandparents.

So come, let us embrace this journey with open hearts and open minds. Let us celebrate the beauty of diversity and the power of love to transform us all. For as we will discover, the unique joy and challenges of having an autistic grandchild can bring us closer to each other, to our community, and to our own true selves.

❖ This Guide Aims to Provide Support, Understanding, and Practical Tips for Grandparents

Being a grandparent enriches our life with love, joy, and purpose. A gift, that is. We have the opportunity to transmit our knowledge, our values, and our heritage to the following generation.. And when we have a grandchild with autism, that gift becomes all the more precious, all the more sacred.

Even while we like our grandchildren, there are times when we don't always know how to raise them and their relatives. We may struggle to understand the unique perspectives and needs of autistic individuals, or to navigate the complex systems and services that are available.

That is why this guide exists. It aims to provide support, understanding, and practical tips for grandparents of autistic children. It is a resource that draws on the wisdom and experiences of experts, advocates, and fellow grandparents, and that offers guidance and inspiration for navigating this journey with love, grace, and resilience.

We shall discuss the benefits and drawbacks of having a grandchild with autism in these pages. We will celebrate the unique strengths and abilities of autistic individuals, and promote a culture of acceptance and inclusion. We will offer practical tips and strategies for supporting your grandchild's development and well-being, and for building a network of support and resources.

We will also address the emotional and practical aspects of navigating this journey, from coping with the initial diagnosis to advocating for systemic change. And throughout it all, we will reiterate the value of love, which serves as the cornerstone of everything we do as grandparents.

So let's start this journey together, don't you dare say. As we celebrate the gift of love that links us all, let's grow together and support one another, and in the world around us.

➢ Understanding Autism

❖ What is Autism?

The journey of autism offers insights into the wonder and complexity of the human mind. It is a singular and wonderful road. Our ability to broaden our perspective of what it means to be human and to acknowledge the myriad ways in which we can view the world will be put to the test on this voyage.

But what precisely is autism? In essence, autism is a neurological condition that limits a person's ability to engage, communicate, and engage in social interactions. For some autistic individuals, these variances may be minimal and controllable. Reevaluate our presumptions.

This chapter will examine the main characteristics of autism and how they affect a person's daily life.rwhelming or uncomfortable. We will examine the social communication differences that can make it difficult to read social cues, understand sarcasm or figurative language, or maintain eye contact.

We will also discuss the repetitive behaviors and routines that can provide comfort and predictability, and the potential for intense interests and passions that can fuel creativity and innovation.And throughout it all, we'll stress how crucial it is to respect autistic people's uniqueness and diversity and to foster an environment of acceptance and inclusion.

So come, let us embark on this journey of understanding autism. Let's embrace the depth and complexity of human variation while also recognizing the special talents and difficulties that autistic people possess. We will discover that the better society we can create for everyone, regardless of their neurodiversity, the more we will understand and love autism.

❖ The Spectrum of Autism

The autism spectrum is a kaleidoscope of colors and patterns, representing the unlimited variety of human experience. This spectrum encourages us to acknowledge the variety and complexity of the human mind by encompassing a wide range of social communication, sensory processing, and behavioral patterns.

There are people at one end of the spectrum who might have minor differences in social communication and sensory processing and who might only need a little help or accommodation. These individuals may be able to build relationships, find employment, and live independently. Also, they could excel in a particular skill or hobby.

The disparities in social communication and sensory processing may be more obvious in those who are on the other end of the spectrum, and they may require more intense care and accommodations. These people could require assistance with a range of life skills, such as daily living, social relationships, and communication.

But, even within this wide range of variants, there are innumerable opportunities for differentiation and nuance. It's possible for certain people to have great talent in fields like math, music, or the arts. Certain people may face unique difficulties, such as co-occurring physical and mental health conditions. Other people, however, could connect their autism to other aspects of their identity, such their gender, culture, or race.

The notion of the autism spectrum is covered in this chapter along with how it impacts our capacity to comprehend and support persons who are autistic. We'll examine the wide range of symptoms associated with autism as well as the different variables that could affect how someone feels.

Come, let's embrace the autism spectrum while recognizing the breadth and depth of human variety. Let's respect the infinite variety of ways we can each view the world while simultaneously acknowledging the unique skills and limitations of each person. We shall observe that the more autistic people we are prepared to welcome, the more we can create a society that is supportive and accepting of everyone, regardless of neurodiversity.

❖ The Diagnostic Process

A family may feel overwhelmed, confused, and uncertain about the future after receiving an autism diagnosis because it can be a challenging and emotional process.It can involve a lot of assessments, evaluations, and consultations with medical professionals, educators, and other experts and demand a significant time, energy, and financial commitment.

The process usually begins with a referral from a doctor or educator who may have seen the person displaying autistic signs or symptoms. A thorough evaluation that includes a range of assessments and tests to gauge the person's cognitive, social, and behavioral functioning may follow this referral.

The diagnostic procedure is not a one-size-fits-all method and may change depending on the age, developmental stage, and other characteristics of the individual. Observation and evaluation of the person's behavior and communication abilities may be part of the process in some circumstances, while more thorough psychological testing may be required in others.

Families should be involved, informed, and encouraged to ask questions and get support as needed throughout the process. To make sure that their needs are met and that they receive the proper services and accommodations, they might need to act as an advocate for their loved one and collaborate closely with healthcare professionals and educators.

The most crucial thing for families to keep in mind is that an autism diagnosis is not a label or a restriction, but rather a chance for understanding, development, and support. It can serve as a framework for comprehending each person's particular strengths and challenges and can direct the creation of tailored strategies and interventions.

So keep in mind that you are not alone if you are starting the diagnostic process for yourself or a loved one. You are a courageous and compassionate caregiver who tries to comprehend and assist your loved one as best you can. And as you proceed on this journey, be aware that you have access to a wealth of resources, support, and advice, and that together we can work to create a world that embraces you.

❖ Debunking Common Myths and Misconceptions

Despite the fact that there are still many myths and misconceptions around the diagnosis of autism, it is a complex and multifaceted condition with a variety of consequences on people. These misconceptions can cause stigma, prejudice, and miscommunication, which can prevent those with autism from getting the help and acceptance they require and merit.

The idea that people with autism lack emotional intelligence or empathy is a common misconception. Simply put, this isn't accurate. Even though it may be true that some people with autism may find it difficult to recognize and express their emotions in the same way as those who are not affected by the condition, these people are still capable of experiencing and expressing a wide range of emotions, including love, joy, and compassion.

The idea that poor or unloving parenting is to blame for autism is another pervasive myth. Because it implies that people with autism or their families are somehow responsible for the disorder, this is a harmful and dangerous misunderstanding. Although the causes of autism are complex and unclear, the autistic person or their loved ones are not to blame.

The idea that every autistic person is the same is a third misconception. Since there are several types of autism, each autistic individual has different needs, challenges, and skills. It's critical to avoid preconceptions and prejudices, approach each person with an open mind, and strive to understand them.

As a last point, keep in mind that people with autism are not limited by their diagnosis. They are complex, multifaceted people who each have their own special skills, interests, and personalities. Children ought to be cherished, supported, and understood if they are to thrive. For their individuality, they deserve respect.

Therefore, if you have an autistic grandchild, it is crucial that you educate yourself on autism and dispel any myths or stereotypes you may encounter. You can do this to support your granddaughter and all people with autism in creating a more accepting and inclusive world.

> ➢ **Communication and Socialization**

❖ **The Importance of Communication and Socialization for Autistic Individuals**

Communication and socialization are essential skills for all individuals, and they are especially important for those with autism. However, for autistic individuals, these skills can often be challenging and require extra support and understanding.

Communication can take many forms, from spoken language to nonverbal cues, and it is important to recognize and respect each individual's unique communication style. Some individuals with autism may struggle with spoken language and prefer alternative methods of communication, such as sign language or picture symbols. Others may have difficulty with social cues and may benefit from explicit instructions and explanations.

In order to interact with people, develop relationships, and create a sense of community, socialization is an important element of existence. However, socializing can be particularly difficult for people with autism as they may find it difficult to comprehend social standards, interpret social signs, and control their emotions in public.

It is important for grandparents of autistic grandchildren to understand and respect their grandchild's unique communication and socialization needs. This may involve learning new communication methods, such as using picture symbols or adapting your communication style to better suit your grandchild's needs. It may also involve providing additional support and guidance in social situations, such as practicing social skills or providing a safe and comfortable environment for social interactions.

By supporting your grandchild's communication and socialization needs, you can help them to build meaningful relationships, connect with others, and develop a strong sense of self-worth and belonging. And by understanding the unique challenges and strengths of individuals with autism, you can create a more inclusive and accepting world for all individuals, regardless of their communication or socialization abilities.

❖ Communication Strategies to Use with Your Grandchild

You are a vital part of your autistic grandchild's life as a grandparent, especially when it comes to communication. For those with autism, communication can be difficult, but with the correct techniques and encouragement, you can support your grandchild in flourishing and realizing their full potential.

Being tolerant and patient is among the most crucial things you can do. Your grandchild may find it more difficult or time-consuming to communicate, but by being patient and empathic in your responses, you can lay a solid foundation of trust and understanding.

Here are some communication strategies that you can use with your grandchild:

1. **Use visual aids** - Many individuals with autism benefit from visual aids, such as pictures, symbols, or written words, to help them understand and communicate. You can create visual aids for everyday tasks or activities, such as a visual schedule or a picture menu for mealtime.

2. **Simplify language** - Use clear, concise language and avoid using idioms or figurative language. Your grandchild may have difficulty understanding abstract concepts or sarcasm, so it's important to be direct and concrete in your communication.

3. **Practice active listening** - When your grandchild is speaking, make sure to give them your full attention and respond with empathy. Repeat back what they have said to ensure that you understand, and ask clarifying questions if needed.

4. **Allow for processing time** - Your grandchild may need extra time to process and respond to your communication. Give them plenty of time to think before expecting a response, and avoid interrupting or finishing their sentences.

5. **Use positive reinforcement** - When your grandchild makes an effort to communicate, whether it be through spoken language, sign language, or other methods, make sure to provide positive reinforcement and praise. This will help to build their confidence and encourage continued communication.

You may make your grandchild feel heard, respected, and supported by employing these techniques and changing your communication style to fit their needs. Remember that communication is a two-way street, and you may develop a close and meaningful bond with your grandchild by being patient and understanding.

❖ How to Support Socialization and Social Skills Development

Autism can make socialization difficult, but your grandchild can learn the social skills necessary to form enduring bonds with others with the correct encouragement and support. The socialization and social skill development of your grandchild can benefit greatly from your help as a grandparent.

Here are some ways that you can help:

1. **Create opportunities for socialization** - Provide opportunities for your grandchild to socialize with others in a safe and encouraging atmosphere, whether through playdates, neighborhood events, or family get-togethers. Encourage them to socialize with others, but don't pressure them if they don't want to.

2. **Model social behavior** - Make important to set a good example for your children since they will observe and mimic your actions. This can involve

doing things like saying hello to people, switching off, and sharing.

3. **Practice social skills -** By engaging in practice with your grandchild, you can aid in the development of their social skills. Role-playing scenarios, such as placing an order at a restaurant or requesting assistance, can boost their self-assurance and prepare children for social interactions in the real world.

4. **Teach empathy -** Empathy is a crucial social skill that people with autism may struggle with. By exhibiting empathy yourself and pointing out how others could be experiencing in certain circumstances, you can teach empathy to others.

5. **Encourage interests -** Encourage your grandchild to explore their passions so they can meet people who have similar interests. This can be a really effective technique to make friends and hone social abilities.

You may assist your grandchild's social skills development by creating a positive and welcoming atmosphere. Remember that socialising involves more than just meeting friends; it also entails developing meaningful connections with other people and engaging in gratifying interactions with them. Your grandchild can acquire the social abilities required to lead a contented life with your love and support.

❖ Tips for Building and Maintaining a Positive Relationship with Your Autistic Grandchild

It can take time and work to develop a good relationship with your autistic grandchild, but the trip can be extremely rewarding for both of you. Here are some pointers to assist you in creating and preserving a good relationship with your grandchild:

1. **Communicate clearly and calmly** - When speaking with your grandchild, be sure to use basic, plain words. Avoid using a strong tone or elevated voice when speaking; some autistic people find these to be overpowering.

2. **Respect their boundaries** - People with autism may struggle with physical touch or sensory overload. Never touch your grandchild without first getting permission from them, and always respect their personal space.

3. **Show interest in their interests** - Express a sincere interest in your grandchild's hobbies and interests. They may feel appreciated and understood as a result of this.

4. **Use positive reinforcement** - A potent strategy for promoting positive behavior is positive reinforcement. Employ tiny prizes or verbal affirmation to reinforce positive actions and accomplishments.

5. **Create a predictable routine** - Predictability and routine are often quite appealing to autistic people. For your visits with your grandchildren, establishing a routine might make them feel more at ease and secure.

6. **Be patient and flexible** - A relationship with an autistic person can take some time and patience to develop. Be accommodating to their requirements, adaptable, and persistent even if it takes some time to see results.

7. **Seek out resources and support** - Grandparents of autistic people can find a lot of resources online. Find support networks, educational materials, and expert advice to aid you during this journey.

Do not forget that developing a good relationship with your autistic grandchild does not mean trying to change who they are. It's about accepting people as they are and demonstrating your love, support, and compassion for them. These pointers will help you create a relationship with your grandchild that will last a lifetime.

➢ Sensory Processing

❖ Understanding Sensory Processing Challenges in Autism

Autism is frequently characterized by difficulties with sensory processing, which can greatly affect a person's daily life. It can be easier for grandparents to support their autistic grandchild if they are aware of these difficulties. Here's what you need to know:

1. **Sensory Overload** - Loud noises, bright lights, and strong smells can cause sensory overload in individuals with autism. Anxiety, frustration, and even discomfort in the body might result from this.

2. **Sensory Under-Responsiveness** - On the other hand, some autistic people may respond less quickly to sensory input, making it challenging for them to recognize or react appropriately to environmental cues.

3. **Sensory Seeking** - Some people with autism actively seek out sensory stimulation like spinning or rocking. This may be a coping strategy to control how they process sensory information.

4. **Sensory Discrimination** - People with autism may struggle to distinguish between various sensory inputs. For instance, they might find it challenging to differentiate between various tastes or textures.

It's crucial for grandparents to understand these difficulties with sensory processing and to provide a safe environment for their grandchildren. Here are some pointers to assist:

1. **Observe and listen** - Spend some time watching your grandchild and paying attention to what they need. Ask them how they are feeling and pay attention to their actions and body language.

2. **Create a sensory-friendly environment** - Reduce triggers in the environment, such as loud noises and bright lights. Consider using sensory tools like weighted blankets or fidget toys and provide comfortable seating.

3. **Respect their sensory preferences** - Respect your grandchild's preferences and give them options if they have sensory preferences, such as a preference for certain smells or textures.

4. **Offer support** - When your grandchild is feeling overwhelmed, support them by encouraging them to express their feelings.

You can assist your grandchild in feeling more at ease and confident in daily life by comprehending and supporting their sensory processing difficulties. In spite of their sensory processing difficulties, they can thrive and realize their full potential with your help and understanding.

❖ Tips for creating a sensory-friendly environment

It's important to think about your autistic grandchild's sensory needs when designing a safe and comfortable environment for them. Following are some pointers for designing a sensory-friendly setting:

1. **Reduce sensory overload:** Keep your home free of clutter and over-the-top decorations because they might overwhelm your grandchild. Instead of using harsh fluorescent lighting, think about using soft lighting.

2. **Provide sensory tools:** To assist your grandchild in regulating their sensory needs, keep items like noise-canceling headphones, weighted blankets, fidget toys, and chewable necklaces on hand.

3. **Use visual supports:** Your grandchild can learn about routines and expectations and experience less stress and confusion by using picture cards, social stories, and visual schedules.

4. **Offer choices:** Give your grandchild options, such as the room they want to be in or the music they want to listen to, so that they can have some control over their surroundings.

5. **Take breaks:** Encourage your grandchild to take a break in a calm, cozy location if they start to feel overwhelmed or overstimulated.

Your grandchild will feel safer and more at ease if you make the environment sensory-friendly. This will also lessen the possibility of sensory overload and meltdowns.

❖ How to recognize and respond to your grandchild's sensory needs

It can be challenging for grandparents to identify and meet the sensory needs of their autistic grandchildren. However, you can create a nurturing and supportive environment by being attentive and empathic. You can identify your grandchild's sensory needs and meet them by using the following advice:

1. **Observe your grandchild:** Observe your grandchild carefully to discover how they respond to various sensory cues. Take note of the smells, sounds, and sensations that seem to reassure or alarm them.

2. **Listen to your grandchild:** Learn what your grandchild needs or desires. When given the chance, autistic people can still communicate their needs, even though they may not always be able to do so in the same way as neurotypical people.

3. **Respond appropriately:** Respond in a way that supports your grandchild's sensory needs once you have determined what they are. If your grandchild, for instance, is bothered by loud noises, try lowering the television's volume or giving them noise-cancelling headphones.

4. **Be patient:** Keep in mind that your grandchild's sensory requirements could change throughout the day or even throughout the minute. Try out various approaches and be patient and adaptable to see what works best for your grandchild.

5. **Seek professional support:** If you are having trouble providing for your grandchild's sensory needs, don't be afraid to seek assistance from a medical professional or therapist who focuses on autism.

You can make a secure and nurturing environment that promotes your grandchild's overall well-being by identifying and attending to their sensory needs.

➤ Education and Advocacy

❖ The role of grandparents in supporting their autistic grandchild's education

You have a significant influence on your autistic grandchild's education as a grandparent. You can provide your grandchild and their parents with invaluable support and direction because of your unique perspective. The different ways you can get involved in your grandchild's education and develop into a strong supporter of their needs are covered in this chapter.

We'll begin by discussing the various learning settings that are accessible to children with autism, such as public schools, private schools, and homeschooling. You'll discover the benefits and drawbacks of each choice and how to collaborate with your grandchild's parents to choose the option that best suits their particular requirements.

The significance of Individualized Education Plans (IEPs) and how they can give your grandchild the support they require to succeed in school will be covered next. You'll learn about the various parts of an IEP and how to work with your grandchild's parents and teachers to develop a thorough plan that satisfies their particular needs.

We'll also talk about how modifications and accommodations can help your grandchild learn and grow in the classroom. You will gain knowledge about how to request modifications that will help your grandchild succeed in their educational setting.

Finally, we'll talk about the value of advocacy and how you can effectively represent the needs of your grandchildren. You will learn about your rights as a grandparent and how to collaborate with the parents and teachers of your grandchild to ensure that their needs are satisfied.

You will have a thorough understanding of the role of grandparents in assisting their autistic grandchild's education by the end of this chapter, as well as the various ways you can have a positive influence on their academic journey.

❖ How to be an effective advocate for your grandchild

Making sure that your autistic grandchild receives the support they require to thrive requires advocacy, which is an essential tool. You can be a huge asset to your grandchild's cause as an advocate because you have a special understanding of their needs as a grandparent. We will look at some advice on how to be a strong grandparent advocate in this chapter.

First and foremost, it's crucial to familiarize yourself with the laws and rules pertaining to special education and disability rights. Your ability to navigate the system and comprehend your grandchild's rights will improve with this knowledge. Participate in meetings with educators and administrators, raise issues, and ask questions. Make sure the individualized education program (IEP) or 504 plan for your grandchild is thorough and contains all required accommodations.

It's also important to establish relationships with the teachers and other adults who will be influencing your grandchild. Work together with them and share your knowledge of what suits your grandchild's needs best. Encourage them to attend training sessions and workshops to deepen their understanding of autism by providing them with resources and research.

It can also be very helpful to connect with other families and people in the autism community. Join support groups, go to events, and take part in online forums to share and learn from the experiences of other families.

Above all, always keep in mind that your grandchild's needs and welfare come first. When necessary, speak up and fight for the things your grandchild needs to succeed. Your grandchild can thrive and reach their full potential with your love and support.

❖ Navigating the educational system and accessing resources

Navigating the educational system and finding the resources your autistic grandchild might require to succeed in school can be overwhelming for grandparents. But you can discover how to be a valuable supporter of your grandchild's education with love, persistence, and patience.

First and foremost, it's crucial to comprehend the special education laws and regulations. Learn about the Individuals with Disabilities Education Act (IDEA) and the rights that apply to your grandchild. Be aware of the various services and accommodations, such as speech therapy, occupational therapy, and individualized instruction that may be available to your grandchild.

Developing a good rapport with your grandchild's teachers and other school staff is also crucial. To keep up with your grandchild's progress and any difficulties they might be facing, attend parent-teacher conferences and other school events. Together with your grandchild's teachers, create a personalized education plan that takes into account all of their special requirements and skills.

To assist autistic people and their families, there are numerous community resources available in addition to working with your grandchild's school. Look for local advocacy, guidance, and service-access organizations and support groups.

Keep in mind that while fighting for your grandchild's educational rights may take persistence and tenacity, the benefits are immeasurable. You can assist your grandchild in realizing their full potential and succeeding in school and beyond by collaborating with their school and utilizing the resources that are available.

❖ Supporting your grandchild's transition to adulthood

You might be concerned about how to help your autistic grandchild make the transition to adulthood as they get older. This chapter aims to offer direction and assistance to grandparents who want to guarantee the best future for their grandchild.

Setting goals, determining strengths and interests, and developing a plan for independent living, post-secondary education, and employment are all components of transition planning, which typically starts in the teenage years. By assisting your grandchild in exploring their options and fighting for their needs, you can play a crucial part in this process as their grandparent.

Some tips for supporting your grandchild's transition include:

1. **Encourage self-advocacy:** It's crucial to teach your grandchild to speak up for themselves as they age. Encourage them to express their preferences and

viewpoints and assist them in acquiring the communication skills they need.

2. **Connect with resources:** Numerous resources are available to help people with autism make the transition to adulthood. Programs for vocational rehabilitation, community-based services, and advocacy groups may all fall under this category. Connect with these resources and consider how they might help your grandchild achieve their objectives.

3. **Explore post-secondary education options:** Many autistic people continue their education beyond high school. Assist your grandchild in evaluating their options and choosing a course that complements their skills and interests.

4. **Support employment goals:** Employment is a crucial aspect of adult life, and with the right support, many people with autism can succeed in the workplace. Assist your grandchild in exploring career options and connecting with services for vocational rehabilitation or job training.

5. **Plan for independent living:** You should think about your grandchild's living situation as they get older. They might need supportive housing or other living arrangements, depending on their needs. Investigate these possibilities and assist your grandchild in acquiring the abilities required for independent living.

The transition to adulthood can be difficult for anyone, but your grandchild can fulfill their dreams with your love and support.

➤ Self-Care for Grandparents

❖ The importance of self-care for grandparents of autistic grandchildren

Dear grandparents,

It's crucial to keep yourself in mind as you navigate the special rewards and difficulties of having an autistic grandchild. The demands of taking care of an autistic grandchild can be too much to handle and can have a negative impact on your physical and mental health.

We will talk about the value of self-care in this chapter and provide helpful advice for caring for yourself as a grandparent of an autistic child. These pointers are intended to assist you in maintaining your own health and wellbeing so that you can continue to give your grandchild the love and support they require.

It's critical to understand that taking care of oneself is not a luxury but rather a necessity. Self-care is not selfish; rather, it is necessary for you to be able to look after your grandchild. Putting off taking care of your needs can result in burnout, stress, and other health issues.

This chapter will discuss the value of establishing boundaries, getting support, practicing self-care, and placing your own physical and mental well-being first. We will also offer helpful advice on how to fit self-care into your schedule despite the demands of looking after a grandchild with autism.

Keep in mind that caring for yourself is a continuous process rather than a one-time event. We hope that this chapter will motivate you to prioritize self-care in your life so that you can continue to give your grandchild the love and care that they require.

Love and strength, those of your grandparents

❖ Strategies for managing stress and maintaining emotional well-being

Grandparenting is a rewarding job, but it can also be difficult, particularly if your grandchild has autism. It's crucial to look after yourself so that you can continue to give your grandchild the love and support they require. We'll look at some methods for controlling stress and preserving emotional health in this chapter.

Making time for self-care is one of the most crucial things you can do for yourself. This could entail taking a soothing bath, going for a stroll, reading a book, or engaging in another enjoyable activity. It's simple to become preoccupied with taking care of your grandchildren, but it's equally important to remember to take care of yourself.

Having a support network is also crucial. This could be a support group for grandparents of autistic children, friends, or family. Talking to people who can relate to what you're going through can be very beneficial. You might also think about seeking out additional support by visiting a therapist or counselor.

You can use other methods in addition to self-care to control stress and preserve your emotional wellbeing. Stress reduction and relaxation can benefit from mindfulness exercises like yoga or meditation. You can feel better physically and mentally with regular exercise and a healthy diet.

Finally, it's critical to keep in mind that asking for assistance is acceptable. Don't be afraid to contact other family members or local resources if you're feeling stressed out or need help caring for your grandchild. The act of asking for assistance is not a sign of weakness.

In conclusion, self-care is a crucial component of being a grandparent, particularly if your grandchild has autism. You can maintain your emotional health and continue to be a loving and supportive influence in your grandchild's life by engaging in self-care, creating a support network, and using stress-management techniques.

❖ How to find support and connect with others in similar situations

It's important to realize that you are not alone in your experience as a grandparent of an autistic grandchild. It's crucial to connect with other grandparents who are traveling the same path as you because they are out there. Your emotional wellbeing can drastically change if you are able to find support and make connections with people who are going through similar things.

Joining online and offline support groups is one way to meet new people. These groups provide a supportive environment where members can talk about their experiences, seek advice, and get emotional support. It's an opportunity to gain new perspectives on how to approach specific circumstances and learn from others who have gone through similar experiences.

Talking to friends and family members is a further means of obtaining support. Sometimes all it takes is for someone to simply listen to your thoughts and feelings. You can start a conversation and get the support you require by letting your loved ones know that you require their understanding and support.

Another crucial component of preserving your emotional wellbeing is self-care. When you're taking care of someone else, it's simple to overlook your own needs, but doing so is counterproductive. Finding enjoyable activities to do, like reading a book, going for a walk, or practicing meditation, can help you feel less stressed and happier overall.

Keep in mind that caring for yourself is not selfish; it is essential for your health and wellbeing. You can support your grandchild more effectively and deal with the difficulties of being a grandparent of an autistic child by seeking out support and taking care of yourself.

➢ Embracing Neurodiversity

❖ The beauty and diversity of the human brain

The human brain is a marvelous and beautiful creation. It is capable of thought, emotion, creation, and interpersonal interaction. However, society has stigmatized people with different brain functions, such as those on the autism spectrum, for far too long.

We will examine the idea of neurodiversity and how it relates to autism in this chapter. We will accept the idea that autism is just a different way of being, rather than seeing it as a disorder or a deficiency. No two brains are alike, just as no two snowflakes are alike, and that is something to be grateful for.

We can make the world more accepting and inclusive of everyone, regardless of differences, by embracing neurodiversity. We can work together to create a society that values diversity and celebrates individuality, and we can learn to value the distinctive perspectives and strengths that autistic people bring to our communities.

Therefore, let's celebrate neurodiversity and all it has to offer. Recognizing the beauty and diversity of the human brain, let's join forces to make a more accepting, inclusive, and compassionate world for everyone.

❖ Understanding the concept of neurodiversity

The appreciation and celebration of the inherent differences in human neurology is known as neurodiversity. It is a theory that questions the idea of normalcy and highlights the importance of diversity. Neurodiversity in the context of autism acknowledges that autistic people have a distinctive and legitimate way of experiencing the world.

It is crucial for grandparents of autistic grandchildren to comprehend and support the idea of neurodiversity. This entails appreciating your grandchild's distinct viewpoint and acknowledging that their neurology differs from your own. It entails giving up trying to treat or fix your grandchild's autism and instead accepting and praising them for who they are.

You can contribute to making the world a more welcoming and inclusive place for your grandchild and all people with autism by embracing neurodiversity. It entails appreciating the beauty and diversity of the human brain and viewing their differences as strengths rather than weaknesses.

❖ How to celebrate and embrace your grandchild's unique strengths and abilities

You have a unique chance to recognize and celebrate your autistic grandchild's special talents and strengths because you are a grandparent. It's critical to keep in mind that neurodiversity is a normal variation in the human brain rather than a disorder or disease.

Focusing on your grandchild's interests and talents is one way to acknowledge their strengths. Nurturing an autistic person's intense passions and interests in a particular subject can give them a sense of purpose and fulfillment. As you show genuine interest in learning more about your grandchild, ask them about their favorite activities or subjects.

Recognizing and appreciating the various perspectives your grandchild has on the world is another way to celebrate neurodiversity. People who are autistic frequently have a distinct viewpoint that can lead to original ideas and creativity. Encourage your grandchild to express themselves creatively through writing, art, or other means.

It's also crucial to acknowledge that people with autism might have various communication preferences and sensory requirements. You can make your grandchild's environment more inclusive and accepting by respecting and accommodating these differences. You might need to modify your communication style, offer sensory-friendly activities or environments, or speak up for your grandchild's needs in social situations like school or other places.

In the end, accepting neurodiversity means accepting your grandchild as they are, with all their special talents and difficulties. You can support your grandchild's development and ensure that they lead happy lives by embracing their diversity and attending to their needs.

❖ Promoting a culture of acceptance and inclusion

You have a special chance to advance an inclusive culture as the grandparent of an autistic child. The first step is to comprehend and embrace neurodiversity, which is the notion that every person has a unique brain and that neurological variations are an inherent aspect of human diversity.

Confronting inaccurate perceptions and attitudes about autism is one way to encourage acceptance and inclusion. Consider your grandchild's autism as a strength rather than a tragedy or a burden, and celebrate those special skills and talents. Encourage other people to follow suit.

Additionally, you can support your grandchild and other autistic people by encouraging inclusion and accessibility in your neighborhood. This could entail promoting sensory-friendly environments, supporting inclusive educational initiatives, or pressuring employers to make accommodations for staff members with autism.

Finally, it's critical to acknowledge and deal with your own biases and presumptions regarding autism. You can foster an environment that is more accepting and inclusive for your grandchild and people who are similar to them by learning more about neurodiversity and challenging your own beliefs.

Remember that celebrating differences is part of embracing neurodiversity, not just accepting and accommodating them. You can ensure that your grandchild and other autistic people are valued and celebrated for who they are by encouraging a culture of acceptance and inclusion.

> ➢ **Navigating Family Dynamics**

❖ **Navigating family dynamics and communicating with family members about your grandchild's autism**

It can be challenging to navigate family dynamics and communicate with other family members about your autistic grandchild's autism as a grandparent. While some family members might be accepting and encouraging, others might find the diagnosis difficult to understand or might even contest it.

Since everyone processes and assimilates information differently, it's critical to approach these discussions with empathy and patience. If you want your family members to understand autism and how it affects your grandchild, you might need to provide education and resources.

As a caregiver, it's crucial to set boundaries and express your needs. In addition, be clear about your expectations for how your grandchild should be treated and accommodated within the family. Don't be afraid to ask for assistance or support when you need it.

In some circumstances, it might be necessary to restrict or terminate communication with relatives who are unable or unwilling to acknowledge your grandchild's autism and offer the necessary support and accommodations. While making this choice can be challenging, it's crucial to put your grandchild's health and safety first.

In some circumstances, it might be necessary to restrict or terminate communication with relatives who are unable or unwilling to acknowledge your grandchild's autism and offer the necessary support and accommodations. While making this choice can be challenging, it's crucial to put your grandchild's health and safety first.

❖ Tips for handling unsupportive or dismissive family members

It can be difficult to navigate family dynamics, particularly when it comes to talking about your grandchild's autism. It's crucial to keep in mind that not everyone may share the same degree of acceptance or understanding, and that's fine. However, coming across family members who are dismissive or unsupportive of your grandchild's diagnosis can still be upsetting and frustrating. Here are some pointers for dealing with these circumstances in an elegant and assured manner.

1. **Educate them:** Sometimes, just because they don't understand autism, family members might not be supportive. Spend some time explaining autism to them and how it affects your grandchild. To give them a better understanding and perspective, share resources and personal stories.

2. **Set boundaries:** Setting boundaries with family members who consistently reject or are not supportive is acceptable. Make it clear to them

what types of behavior are unacceptable and what will happen if they continue to act inappropriately.

3. **Focus on the positive:** While dwelling on the negative actions of unsupportive family members can be easy, it's important to also pay attention to those who are accepting and supportive. Keep your grandchild and you in the company of inspiring people, and turn to them for assistance when necessary.

4. **Seek outside support:** It can occasionally be beneficial to look for outside support, like from a therapist or support group. These resources can give you a safe place to express your feelings and worries while also offering advice and support on how to deal with difficult family dynamics.

Keep in mind that you are not traveling alone. It may be difficult to deal with relatives who aren't willing to help you and your grandchild, but there are plenty who are loving, accepting, and ready to do so. Regardless of the difficulties that may arise, keep your attention on the good things and keep fighting for your grandchild's needs.

❖ How to promote understanding and acceptance within the family

Autism has an impact on the whole family as well as the person who has been diagnosed. As a grandparent, you might discover that some family members find it difficult to accept your grandchild's special needs and behaviors as well as their autism. When there is a lack of acceptance or understanding in the family, it can be difficult to navigate the dynamics, but there are things you can do to encourage acceptance and understanding.

Education is one means of fostering acceptance and comprehension. Your family members can learn more about autism and its symptoms from you. You can describe how it impacts your grandchild and how people can help. It's critical to approach these discussions with tolerance and empathy, keeping in mind that not everyone will immediately comprehend or accept your grandchild's autism.

Personal narratives are yet another means of fostering acceptance and understanding. Helping others understand what it's like to live with the condition can be facilitated by sharing your personal experiences with your grandchild and their autism. It can also aid in dispelling myths and stereotypes about autism.

Setting boundaries with relatives who are unsupportive of or dismissive of your grandchild's needs is also very important. You can explain to them what actions are prohibited and how they can help your grandchild. It's crucial to express these boundaries in a composed manner, and to be ready to uphold them if necessary.

Finally, encouraging a culture of inclusion also entails fostering mutual respect and acceptance within the family. Family members should be urged to include your grandchild in activities and to take special care of their special needs. Encourage them to realize that your grandchild's differences do not diminish their value or their deservingness of your love and acceptance.

Keep in mind that it takes time and patience to foster tolerance and acceptance within the family. Be ready for opposition and misunderstandings, but also be receptive to discussions and chances for improvement. You can give your grandchild and your family as a whole a supportive and accepting environment by working together.

➢ Helping Your Grandchild Thrive

❖ Practical tips and strategies for supporting your grandchild's development and well-being

You only want the best for your autistic grandchild as their grandparent. You want to support their growth and wellbeing in any way you can because you want to see them prosper. Fortunately, you can help your grandchild thrive by using a variety of useful advice and techniques.

1. **Focus on your grandchild's strengths:** Focusing on your grandchild's strengths is one of the best ways to ensure their success. You can help your grandchild gain confidence and feel valued by highlighting and supporting the special talents and skills that each autistic person possesses.

2. **Create a predictable routine:** Many autistic people benefit from predictability and routine. Your grandchild may feel safer and more at ease in their surroundings if you establish a routine that is structured and predictable. Make an effort to establish regular daily schedules for your meals, bedtime, and other activities.

3. **Use visual aids and schedules:** For those with autism, visual aids and schedules can be very beneficial because they offer a straightforward and predictable method of conveying information. To help your grandchild understand what is expected

of them and what will happen next, think about using picture schedules, visual checklists, or other visual aids.

4. **Provide opportunities for sensory input:** There are difficulties with sensory processing for many autistic people, as we covered in earlier chapters. For your grandchild, offering opportunities for sensory input can be very beneficial. This might involve sports like swinging, trampoline jumping, or using sensory toys.

5. **Foster independence:** While it's crucial to support and mentor your grandchild, it's also crucial to encourage their independence. Encourage your grandchild to take on responsibility that is appropriate for their age and to venture out on their own. Their sense of confidence and independence may increase as a result.

6. **Encourage communication and socialization:** Many autistic people find it difficult to communicate and interact with others, but these are essential abilities for forming relationships and surviving in the outside world. Encourage your grandchild to express their needs and emotions, and give them chances to interact with other kids.

7. **Advocate for your grandchild:** As we covered in earlier chapters, advocacy is crucial for promoting the growth and wellbeing of your grandchild. Prepare yourself to speak up for your grandchild's needs and to collaborate with their educators and

medical professionals to make sure they get the help and resources they require.

8. **Take care of yourself:** Finally, remember to look after yourself as well. Taking care of a grandchild with autism can be difficult and demanding, so it's crucial to put yourself first. Remember to take breaks, ask for help when you need it, and place a high priority on your own physical and mental well-being.

In conclusion, there are a variety of doable advice and methods you can employ to promote the growth and wellbeing of your autistic grandchild. You can support your grandchild to thrive and realize their full potential by putting an emphasis on their strengths, establishing a predictable routine, using visual aids and schedules, offering opportunities for sensory input, fostering independence, encouraging communication and socialization, speaking up for your grandchild, and taking care of yourself.

❖ How to Create a Supportive and Nurturing Environment for Your Grandchild

You have a crucial part to play in providing your autistic grandchild with a nurturing and supportive environment. You can support them in flourishing and developing into self-assured, competent adults by being aware of their particular needs and strengths. We'll look at some useful advice in this chapter for raising your grandchild in a nurturing and supportive environment.

1. **Create a safe and predictable space:** Children with autism frequently have trouble adjusting to sudden changes and surprises. Your grandchild will feel safer and more secure if you make the environment predictable and safe. Keep their surroundings as consistent as you can, with a dependable routine and recognizable objects nearby.

2. **Offer plenty of opportunities for sensory exploration:** Your autistic grandchild can explore their senses and learn new skills by engaging in sensory play. Soft blankets, textured balls, and musical instruments are just a few examples of the many textures, colors, and sounds you can provide for them to play with.

3. **Encourage communication and socialization:** The overall development and wellbeing of your grandchild depends on communication and socialization. Offer a lot of opportunities for social interaction with other people, both adults and

children, and encourage them to communicate with you and those around them.

4. **Use visual supports:** Your autistic grandchild may benefit from visual supports like pictures and symbols to better understand their surroundings and express their needs. You can make picture cards to help them express their needs and wants or visual schedules to help them understand their daily schedule.

5. **Practice patience and understanding:** Autism-related needs and modes of interaction with the world are frequently peculiar in children. It's critical to exercise tolerance and comprehension as they deal with these difficulties. Try to understand the world from their point of view, and be adaptable in how you respond to their requirements.

6. **Celebrate their strengths and accomplishments:** No matter how minor they may seem, it's important to acknowledge your grandchild's strengths and accomplishments. Praise for their accomplishments can boost their self-esteem and confidence while also motivating them to keep learning and developing.

You can support your autistic grandchild to thrive and realize their full potential by providing a loving and supportive environment. Always remember to treat their individual needs with patience, understanding, and an open heart, and to recognize and celebrate their successes along the way.

❖ Advocating for your grandchild's needs and promoting their independence

Being an advocate for your grandchild's needs and fostering their independence are both important roles for grandparents of autistic grandchildren to play. This can be a tricky balance to strike, but with love, persistence, and an open mind, you can support your grandchild's development. Here are some pointers for promoting your grandchild's independence while also speaking up for them:

1. **Educate Yourself:** To effectively advocate for your grandchild, you must first become knowledgeable about autism and their particular needs. Attend workshops, read books, and speak with experts who assist people with autism. The more you know, the more effectively you can speak up for your grandchild.

2. **Collaborate with Professionals:** Working together with experts, such as therapists, physicians, and educators, can be beneficial in promoting your grandchild's interests. These experts possess the skills and knowledge necessary to assist your grandchild in realizing their full potential.

3. **Understand Your Grandchild's Needs and Strengths:** Spend some time getting to know your grandchild's unique needs and abilities. This will enable you to represent them in a way that is specific to their particular circumstances. Celebrate

their accomplishments and assist them in overcoming any difficulties they may encounter.

4. **Encourage Independence:** For the sake of fostering your grandchild's growth and development, it's critical to encourage independence. Simply encouraging those to dress themselves or prepare their own meals can accomplish this. No matter how minor they may seem, congratulate them on their achievements.

5. **Foster Self-Advocacy:** Encourage your grandchild to become their own advocate as they get older. Encourage them to speak up for themselves by teaching them how to express their needs and desires. They will grow important skills and be prepared for adulthood as a result of this.

6. **Create a Support Network:** Making a support system for your grandchild can help you speak up for their needs. Make contact with other families who have autistic children to exchange information and resources. Additionally, this may help you and your grandchild emotionally.

7. **Be Persistent:** It can take a while and be challenging to fight for your grandchild. Be persistent in looking for the tools and assistance they require. Do not hesitate to ask for help or to speak up if you feel that your grandchild's needs are not being met.

Every child is different, so there isn't a one-size-fits-all strategy for supporting your grandchild. You can support your grandchild in flourishing and realizing their full potential by being understanding, persistent, and patient.

➢ Epilogue

❖ Reflecting on the journey of being a grandparent to an autistic grandchild

You might experience a range of emotions as you consider your journey as a grandparent of an autistic grandchild. Although there may have been times when you felt frustrated, perplexed, or even heartbroken, there were also times when you felt joy, wonder, and a great deal of pride in the advancement your grandchild has made.

Even though you may have needed to make your way through the unknown, look for help, and speak up for your grandchild's needs, you have always been a dependable source of love and support. You have stood up for the wellbeing, development, and growth of your grandchild.

Being supportive of the difficulties and benefits that come with having an autistic grandchild requires a special kind of person. You've shown that you're kind, patient, and open to changing as you go.

You have undoubtedly learned more from your grandchild than you could have ever imagined about fortitude, creativity, and the wonder of the human mind. You have personally experienced an autistic person's distinctive strengths and abilities, and you have grown to respect the variety of the human experience.

Continue to recognize your grandchild's achievements and fight for their needs as you go forward. Keep in mind that your love and support will always be a source of strength for your grandchild and cherish the times when you are able to connect and feel joy.

When you look back on your experience raising a grandchild with autism, you may find that you have developed and learned more than you ever imagined. You have evolved into a pillar of affection and strength, an inspiration to others, and a beloved relative in your grandchild's life.

❖ The love, joy, and lessons learned along the way

As the process of raising a grandchild with autism comes to an end, it's time to reflect on the love, joy, and lessons learned.

Grandparenting a grandchild with autism can undoubtedly present unique challenges and difficulties, but it can also be a happy and loving journey. Seeing your grandchild develop and become the amazing person they were meant to be is truly beautiful.

Along the way, you have learned a lot about the world, your grandchild, and yourself. You now appreciate the importance of tolerance, understanding, and empathy. On behalf of your grandchild, you now have the knowledge necessary to advocate for, support, and navigate the complex educational and healthcare systems.

But most importantly, you now know what true love is really all about. You have seen how love can bind people together, overcome obstacles, and create a bond that nothing can break.

As you consider this journey, a variety of emotions might come to mind. Maybe there were times of disappointment, sadness, or even rage. There have, however, also been moments of pure joy, pride, and love.

The fact that you supported your grandchild through every stage is ultimately what matters the most. By demonstrating your respect and appreciation for them as they are, you have also given them the assurance that you will always be there for them, no matter what.

Think back on the love, joy, and lessons you learned as you say goodbye to this time in your life. Accept the successes, setbacks, and experiences. Most importantly, keep in mind the love that first drew you and your grandchild together.

❖ Encouragement and support for other grandparents embarking on this journey

To my fellow grandparents on this journey,

I am thankful for the love and joy that my grandchild has brought into my life as I reflect on my experience as a grandparent of an autistic grandchild. I have discovered a great deal about my grandchild, myself, and the rest of the world through all of the ups and downs, struggles and triumphs.

I want to support and encourage you as you go down this path. Understand that you are not alone and that there is a community of grandparents who can offer assistance and compassion because they have gone through similar experiences.

Celebrate your grandchild's successes and landmarks, no matter how insignificant they may seem, and appreciate the unique skills and abilities that only your grandchild possesses. Create a nurturing and encouraging environment, speak up for their needs, and support their independence.

Keep in mind that you must take care of yourself as well, and find the tools and assistance you require to deal with any stress or difficulties that may arise. Above all, remember the influence that love can have on the life of your grandchild.

I am appreciative of the lessons I have gained from this experience and wish to use it to comfort and enlighten others who are beginning a similar journey.

Love and strength,

= THE END =

We appreciate you selecting this book! We hope your expectations were fulfilled or surpassed.

Please think about posting a review on social media if you liked our book. We value your opinion because it enables us to make improvements to our goods and services for future clients.

We want to thank you once more for your support and send our best to you.

PUBLISHING

Follow Us to Stay Updated on New Releases

 We offer our eBooks for free during the initial launch period. By following us, you will be among the first to know when a new eBook is released and have the opportunity to download it completely free of charge.

Don't miss out on our latest releases! Simply click on the link below, follow us, and stay up-to-date on all of our new eBooks.

amazon.com/author/as-publishing

Printed in Great Britain
by Amazon

27122848R00036